Reading Comprehension

Level 2

Series Designer
Philip J. Solimene

Editor
Sharon Diane Orlan

Reading Consultant
Sidney J. Rauch, Ed.D.
Professor of Reading and Education
Hofstra University, New York

EDCON

Story Authors
Linda Bosson
Jackson Daviss
Linda Gillen
Camille Harper
Heather Hellenbrand
Justine Kusner
Geraldine Marie

Copyright © 1997
A/V Concepts Corp.
30 Montauk Blvd, Oakdale NY 11769
info@edconpublishing.com
1-888-553-3266
Visit our Web site at: www.edconpublishing.com

Printed in U.S.A.
ISBN# 0-931334-46-2

CONTENTS

CONTENTS

Ginger's New Home

Learn the Key Words

quick	(kwik)	very fast; able to do something in a short time *The deer in the forest were <u>quick</u> to get away.*
race	(rās)	1. a contest of speed *There was a <u>race</u> to see who was the fastest runner.* 2. to run very quickly *She had to <u>race</u> to catch the bus.*
rode	(rōd)	past tense of ride; to have been carried by or on something *Peter <u>rode</u> on the pony at the farm.*
sled	(sled)	a toy or wagon used for carrying people or things on ice or snow *We used a <u>sled</u> to get down the snow-covered hill.*
start	(stärt)	to begin to move or do something *When the whistle blows, the race will <u>start</u>.*
station	(stā ′ shən)	• a stopping place *The train got to the <u>station</u> on time.*

Preview:
1. Read the title.
2. Look at the picture.
3. Read the first four paragraphs of the story.
4. Then answer the following question.

You learned from your preview that
____a. Steven's father bought Mr. Winn's farm.
____b. Ginger was the name of Steven's new pony.
____c. Ginger was a cow.
____d. Steven's father and Mr. Winn did not like
      each other.

Turn to the Comprehension Check on page 4 for the right answer.

Now read the story.
Read to find out how Steven solves a problem.

1

Ginger's New Home

Steven is very happy about getting a new pony, but is in for some surprises.

Ginger's New Home

Steven sat next to his father in their truck. They had just passed the railroad station. They were on their way to Mr. Winn's farm. This was the day that Steven was to get his own pony.

When they got to the farm, Steven was quick to get out of the truck. He said "Hello" to Mr. Winn and ran quickly over to the barn. Then he saw Ginger. She was under the apple tree, standing with the cows.

He called to her. When she heard him, she ran very quickly to her new friend.

Mr. Winn told Steven, "You must learn how to care for Ginger before you start to ride her."

He showed Steven how to hold Ginger, and many other things. Then Mr. Winn put Steven on Ginger's back and they both rode away.

Ginger did not go very quickly. After all, she wasn't in a race. They rode past the railroad station, and when it got late, they started back to Steven's house.

That night, Steven thought of lots of things that he and Ginger could do together. She could pull a sled for him in the winter. Yes, he could even picture it now—a big red sled and a blanket around Ginger's back. They could race around the old barnyard near his home and chase the chickens and cows.

The next morning, Steven went out to ride Ginger. She was not in the barn or in the field. Steven called to her, but she didn't come running.

Then he saw that the fence was down.

"Oh no!" he shouted. "Ginger has run away!"

"We'll go look for her," said his father, as he started the truck.

They drove for a long time, but could not find her. Then they drove to Mr. Winn's farm.

"Look!" shouted Steven. "There she is!"

His father stopped the truck and Steven jumped out. He raced over to the apple tree. Ginger was there, right in the middle of all of the cows.

As Mr. Winn and Steven's father walked over, Steven said to his father, "I guess Ginger is just homesick."

Then Mr. Winn told them, "When Ginger was growing up, she was around the cows all the time. She has gotten very used to them being around her."

"Well," said Steven's father, "I guess we're going to have to let Ginger meet our cows."

So Steven rode Ginger back to his house, while his father drove. When they got home, Steven and Ginger rode into the field where the cows were. Ginger looked happy. When Steven went to bed that night, Ginger was still with her new friends.

The next day, Steven dressed quickly and ran to the field. He looked all around and then he saw something that made him laugh. The cows were coming over the hill, and Ginger was right in the middle of the group!

Yes, she would be very happy in her new home.

Ginger's New Home

COMPREHENSION CHECK

Choose the best answer.

1. At Mr. Winn's farm Steven got a
_____a.   cow.
_____b.   pony.
_____c.   sled.
_____d.   chicken.

2. Steven
_____a.   knew everything about cows.
_____b.   wanted to get a bigger horse.
_____c.   had to learn about horses.
_____d.   liked race horses better than ponies.

3. The story takes place
_____a.   in a house.
_____b.   on a boat.
_____c.   in a forest.
_____d.   on a farm.

4. After Mr. Winn showed Steven a few things about Ginger,
_____a.   Steven rode Ginger back to his farm.
_____b.   Steven brought Ginger home in the truck.
_____c.   Mr. Winn put Ginger on a train.
_____d.   Mr. Winn walked Ginger to Steven on a rope.

5. When Steven went out to ride Ginger the next morning,
_____a.   Ginger was not in the field or the barn.
_____b.   he took her for a visit to Mr. Winn's house.
_____c.   Ginger was hiding in the barn.
_____d.   Steven's father was bathing her.

6. Steven and his father
_____a.   looked all day and couldn't find Ginger.
_____b.   waited at the farm for Ginger to come home.
_____c.   found Ginger at Mr. Winn's farm.
_____d.   were happy that Ginger could jump high.

7. Ginger
_____a.   liked to play with the sheep.
_____b.   felt at home with the cows.
_____c.   only wanted to jump the fence.
_____d.   did not like to eat apples.

8. After Ginger met Steven's cows, she
_____a.   was happy in her new home.
_____b.   still ran away to Mr. Winn's farm.
_____c.   became fresh and kicked Steven.
_____d.   never ate anything but grass.

9. Another name for this story could be
_____a.   "When the Cows Come Home."
_____b.   "A Funny Pony."
_____c.   "Mr. Winn's Farm."
_____d.   "The Land of the Lost Horses."

10. This story is mainly about
_____a.   a young boy who is afraid of horses.
_____b.   learning all about a new pony.
_____c.   a father who is always away from home.
_____d.   a friendly neighbor with horses and cows.

Check your answers with the key on page 53.

Idea Starter: How is Steven and his family like yours? How are they different?

Ginger's New Home

VOCABULARY CHECK

quick	race	rode	sled	start	station

I. *Fill in the blank in each sentence with the right word from the box above.*

1. The train stopped at every_____along the way.

2. Mom was_____to drop the hot plate.

3. We took our_____to the top of the snowy hill.

4. The fastest horse won the_____.

5. We don't_____eating until everyone is sitting at the table.

6. Paul_____in the wagon all the way to school.

II. *Use the words from the box above to fill in the spaces in the story below.*

It was time for Steven to_____back to his father's farm with his new pony. He and

Ginger_____past the railroad_____. Steven thought of how Ginger could

pull his_____in the winter. They would_____against other ponies at the fair

in the summer. Steven was_____to love his new friend.

Check your answers with the key on page 55.

Max the Moose

Learn the Key Words

quiet	(kwī ′ ət)	without noise *The room was quiet after everyone went home.*
ring	(ring)	1. a noise made by a bell *We heard the doorbell ring.* 2. a circle of people or things *We stood in a ring around the fire.* 3. a piece of jewelry worn on a finger *I got a gold ring for my birthday.*
sell	(sel)	to give away for money *The girls will sell lemonade and cookies for 10 cents.*
skate	(skāt)	to move or race on ice; a special kind of shoe *I do not know how to ice skate, but I would like to learn.*
suppose	(sə pōz ′)	to think of what might be *Do you suppose it will rain?*
teach	(tēch)	to show how something is done; to help *Bob wanted to teach his brother a new game.*

Preview:
1. Read the title.
2. Look at the picture.
3. Read the first four paragraphs of the story.
4. Then answer the following question.

You learned from your preview that
____a. Gerard and his grandfather liked to do things together.
____b. Gerard's grandfather was teaching him to skate.
____c. Max the Moose went skating with Gerard.
____d. Gerard's grandfather wanted to sell his fish.

Turn to the Comprehension Check on page 9 for the right answer.

Now read the story.
Read to find out about a friendly forest animal.

Max the Moose

Gerard's grandfather is an interesting old man who tells some very good stories. He also has some rather interesting friends.

Some Things You Will Read About:

antlers (ant ′ lərs) a horn-like growth on the head of an animal
moose (müs)   a large animal, like a deer

Max the Moose

It was a quiet, cold day in the woods. Gerard and his grandfather sat by the warm fire. They liked to be together. For a long time, they had wanted to go to the lake to skate and to fish. And today they had done just that. They would eat some of the fish and maybe sell the rest. Now Gerard's grandfather was about to teach him how to make a pipe out of wood.

Suddenly, through the quiet woods, they heard the ring of a small bell.

"What do you suppose that is?" Gerard asked quickly.

"That's Max the moose," his grandfather said.

Well, when Gerard heard the name Max the moose, he wanted to know all about him. So his grandfather began to tell him about Max.

Gerard's grandfather said that when he was a boy, he,too, went to the forest with *his* grandfather. They had just been skating and fishing at the lake. Their skates were hanging from a tree. The fish they had caught were in a big red pail. They were going to eat some fish and then sell the rest.

Then Gerard's grandfather came to the part of his story that would teach Gerard about

what could happen in the forest.

He told Gerard that they had turned their backs for just a minute. Suddenly, a large animal came out of the dark forest. It took the pail of fish!

"What do you suppose it was?" Gerard's grandfather asked.

"It was Max!" shouted Gerard. "Max the moose!"

Gerard's grandfather said it was Max for sure. Max loved fish. But they weren't going to let Max get away with taking their dinner. Max ran quickly through the woods. But so did they. Soon they found Max in a clear part of the woods. He was eating the fish.

All of a sudden, they heard the sound of a wild animal. They turned around and saw a large bear coming towards them.

They climbed the nearest tree as fast as they could. Then they watched Max and the bear from the tree. Max made a very loud moose call. The bear was so afraid, that he turned and ran away. Max was very happy with himself.

"But what about the fish?" Gerard asked.

Gerard's grandfather said that first they came down from

the tree. Then they walked over to Max. They took half of the fish and gave the rest to Max because he had saved them. Max was so happy that he wagged his tail. Before they left,they tied a bell to one of Max's antlers.

"This way we would always know which moose was Max, and which moose should share our fish," Gerard's grandfather said.

And to this day, whenever you hear a bell ring in the forest, you can be sure that it's Max.

Max the Moose

COMPREHENSION CHECK

Choose the best answer.

1. Gerard and his grandfather were
   ____a. selling pipes near the lake.
   ____b. skating and fishing.
   ____c. looking for a moose.
   ____d. on their way home.

2. The bell that Gerard heard was on a
   ____a. train.
   ____b. bike.
   ____c. moose.
   ____d. man.

3. Gerard's grandfather
   ____a. saw Max for the first time,with Gerard.
   ____b. was afraid that Max would hurt Gerard.
   ____c. didn't want Max to have any fish.
   ____d. met Max when he was a young boy.

4. Gerard
   ____a. had fun with his grandfather.
   ____b. didn't like to fish and swim.
   ____c. couldn't wait to get home.
   ____d. did not care about the moose.

5. Max
   ____a. liked to visit Gerard's grandfather by the lake.
   ____b. had taken grandfather's fish years before.
   ____c. never came near anyone in the woods.
   ____d. always went swimming at the lake.

6. As Max was eating the fish,
   ____a. Gerard's grandfather took them away.
   ____b. a bear frightened him away.
   ____c. Gerard's grandfather brought him some more.
   ____d. a bear came towards them .

7. The moose
   ____a. killed the bear.
   ____b. ran quickly away.
   ____c. never came back again.
   ____d. saved Gerard's grandfather.

8. In order to thank Max, Gerard's grandfather
   ____a. took the moose home.
   ____b. always shared his fish with the moose.
   ____c. bought the moose a present.
   ____d. made the moose a small house.

9. Another name for this story could be
   ____a. "The Bell in the Woods."
   ____b. "A Day With Grandparents."
   ____c. "Making Pipes."
   ____d. "Learning to Skate."

10. This story is mainly about
    ____a. the tale of a lovable moose.
    ____b. the lake in the woods.
    ____c. a grandfather's life.
    ____d. what young boys do.

Check your answers with the key on page 53.

Idea Starter: Which animal do you think is most interesting and why?

Max the Moose

VOCABULARY CHECK

quiet	ring	sell	skate	suppose	teach

I.   Fill in the blank in each sentence with the correct word from the box above.

1.   We heard the doorbell_____and we knew we had company.

2.   The children were very_____when the show started.

3.   I_____John will come to the party after the ball game.

4.   We_____cold drinks in the summer.

5.   My brother likes to_____me how to throw a ball.

6.   I_____on the icy lake in winter.

II.   Find the words from the box above that are hidden in the puzzle below and circle each one. One word, which is not a key word, has been done for you.

```
L Q U I E T M
B A K E E M T
S U P P O S E
K O R W S K A
A V I R E P C
T B N Z L S H
E K G M L R V
```

Check your answers with the key on page 55.

This page may be reproduced for classroom use.

THE SECRET OF THE MAGIC WATER

Learn the Key Words

afternoon	(af tər nün´)	the time of the day after twelve noon and before evening *Johnny played baseball this afternoon.*
between	(bi twēn´)	space keeping two people or things apart *Jack walked between Mary and Sam.*
careful	(kar´ fəl)	done or said with thought; with care *Sally was careful not to break the glass dish.*
eight	(āt)	the number after seven *Susan has eight pairs of shoes.*
kick	(kik)	to hit with the foot *Billy can kick a football far.*
magic	(maj´ ik)	clever tricks *The book fell off the table as if by magic.*

Preview:
1. Read the title.
2. Look at the picture.
3. Read the first four paragraphs of the story.
4. Then answer the following question.

You learned from your preview that
_____a. it had been raining for weeks.
_____b. the sky was full of clouds.
_____c. the creek and the land were bone dry.
_____d. Johnny and Billy lived in the same village.

Turn to the Comprehension Check on page 14 for the right answer.

Now read the story.
Read to find out about two boys who solve a big problem.

THE SECRET OF THE MAGIC WATER

Why has the creek dried up and what will Johnny and Billy discover when they try to find out?

Some Things You Will Read About:

secret	(sē′ krit)	something hidden; not to be told to others
spirit	(spir′ it)	something that is not real, but makes itself known
trap	(trap)	hidden door or something that catches things
village	(vil′ ij)	a group of houses

THE SECRET OF THE MAGIC WATER

Billy Morgan watched his best friend, Johnny Longspear, kick a stone across the yard. Puffs of brown dust rose all around the stone. There had been no rain. The creek that watered Johnny's farm and sheep had dried up. There were eight other families who lived near the creek. And their land and animals did not have water.

Billy's father taught at the school in the Indian village. He did not know why the creek had dried up. Johnny's grandfather said the water was magic and that a bad spirit had stolen it.

Billy looked at the cloudless, afternoon sky.

"I've got to go, Johnny," he said. "My father wants me to help with some chores."

Johnny kicked another stone. "O.K. See you tomorrow, Billy," he said.

When Billy got home, his father was watering the corn from the water tank. He was careful to let out just enough water. Billy wished that Johnny's grandfather had a water tank like theirs. The big tank had a trap door in it. When Mr. Morgan opened the trap door, the water ran between the rows of corn.

Suddenly, Billy wondered if someone had put the magic water in a tank. If so, maybe he and Johnny could ask the person to let some of the water go. Billy could hardly wait to tell Johnny his plan.

Johnny was glad too. "We can ride our ponies up the mountain tomorrow afternoon," he told Billy. "Then we can find out about the magic water."

The next afternoon, Billy saddled Popcorn. Soon he moved him into a fast walk. Johnny was riding Two Spot, his best pony. Then, the two boys started up the mountain. They had to be very careful of the rocky ground.

At first, they rode with the creek between them. Then they had to ride single file. Now they had to get off their ponies and lead them. They were high above the Indian village.

When they came to a big rock, they had to walk their ponies past it. And, right behind it, lay the secret of the magic water!

A large tree trunk had fallen across the creek, and it was stopping the water from running. Just like the trap door in Billy's water tank!

Billy and Johnny tried to move the trunk, but they just couldn't.

"The ponies!" shouted Billy. "We can move the trunk with the ponies and ropes."

Quickly, the boys tied one end of their ropes to the trunk and the other to the saddles. The ponies pulled at the ropes and the trunk moved! The boys yelled at the ponies to pull harder. The ponies dug in their hooves and the trunk pulled free.

"We did it!" yelled Johnny.

The water rushed down the mountain. Soon it would reach Johnny's grandfather and the eight other families.

The two boys rode home. Johnny's grandfather gave a big party for Billy and Johnny and their brave ponies. They had run the bad spirit off. And they had found the secret of the magic water.

THE SECRET OF THE MAGIC WATER

COMPREHENSION CHECK

Choose the best answer.

1. The farms in the Indian village were very dry because
____a. it was a very hot summer.
____b. the creek had dried up.
____c. Billy's father had all the water.
____d. someone else bought the creek.

2. A water tank
____a. finds water.
____b. makes water.
____c. stores water.
____d. carries away water.

3. Watching his father's tank gave Billy the idea
____a. to let out the water for Johnny.
____b. that the water in the creek might be trapped.
____c. to get the trunk loose.
____d. that his pony needed water from the tank.

4. Billy and Johnny
____a. told their fathers to go look for the creek.
____b. stayed home from school to look for water.
____c. walked to the creek to find the magic.
____d. went along the creek to see what was wrong.

5. Popcorn and Two Spot were the names of
____a. ponies.
____b. Indian braves.
____c. dogs.
____d. rivers.

6. The water in the creek had stopped running because
____a. there was none left.
____b. it was bad magic.
____c. a trunk had fallen in its path.
____d. it was dried up.

7. Billy and Johnny got the water free by
____a. calling for help.
____b. getting a wagon and pulling.
____c. asking their families to help.
____d. using their ponies and ropes.

8. The Indian people believed that the water was magic because it
____a. kept everything growing and alive.
____b. was kept in big tanks.
____c. kept them from getting sick.
____d. never stopped running.

9. Another name for this story could be
____a. "Water Tanks Save Lives."
____b. "Trouble at the Creek."
____c. "Two Lost Ponies."
____d. "Life in the Village."

10. This story is mainly about
____a. looking for a magic well.
____b. going to school in an Indian village.
____c. finding out why something is happening.
____d. the way Indians lived long ago.

Check your answers with the key on page 53.

Idea Starter: What do you think would have happened if the boys didn't find out what was wrong?

THE SECRET OF THE MAGIC WATER

VOCABULARY CHECK

afternoon	between	careful	eight	kick	magic

I.   Fill in the blank in each sentence with the right word from the box above.

1.   I go to the park every_____ .

2.   Be_____not to drop this glass.

3.   _____is one more than seven.

4.   I wanted to_____the can, but I picked it up instead.

5.   We like to walk_____our mother and father.

6.   At the_____show, a bird was pulled out of a hat.

II.   Are the key words used correctly? Check yes or no.

1.   To be <u>careful</u> is to think about what you are doing.   _____Yes   _____No

2.   <u>Eight</u> is one more than six.   _____Yes   _____No

3.   When you <u>kick</u> something you pick it up.   _____Yes   _____No

4.   If you are <u>between</u> two children you are keeping them apart.   _____Yes   _____No

5.   It is always dark in the <u>afternoon</u>.   _____Yes   _____No

6.   <u>Magic</u> is clever tricks and puzzles.   _____Yes   _____No

Check your answers with the key on page 56.

Barry and Chuck at Camp

Learn the Key Words

asleep   (ə slēp′)   sleeping
Mary fell asleep in her favorite chair.

begin   (bi gin′)   start
When will we begin to play the game?

camp   (kamp)   a place in the country for vacation where tents and cabins are used
Bobby will go to camp for the summer.

flag   (flag)   a piece of cloth with special colors; something which stands for a special place or thing
The flag of the country was flying in the wind.

kept   (kept)   past tense of keep; to have and not let go
Cindy kept the cookies for herself.

mail   (māl)   letters or things that are sent
Tommy got two letters in the mail.

Preview:
1. Read the title.
2. Look at the picture.
3. Read the first five paragraphs of the story.
4. Then answer the following question.

You learned from your preview that
____a. Mr. Stanley was the mailman.
____b. Barry's sister wrote a letter to Chuck.
____c. Barry got a postcard.
____d. Harry got a box of cookies from home.

Turn to the Comprehension Check on page 19 for the right answer.

Now read the story.
Read to find out about a strange happening at camp.

Barry and Chuck at Camp

When Barry and Chuck go to camp, they have lots of fun and interesting adventures.

Barry and Chuck at Camp

Barry and Chuck were asleep in their sleeping bags when they heard someone yell out, "The mail is here, boys!" It was Mr. Stanley who was in charge at Camp Tummy Too.

Barry and Chuck ran to the flagpole where Mr. Stanley stood holding the mail.

"Well, boys, I'm going to begin giving out the mail," Mr. Stanley said. "Oscar, here are two letters for you and Harry, here's a box from home, maybe it's cookies. Here's a postcard for you Barry and a letter for Chuck."

Both Barry and Chuck began to read their mail.

"It's just a card from my sister," said Barry. Then he read it aloud:

Dear Barry,

I'm having more fun than you at camp. Today we went on a picnic and then a boat ride. Tomorrow, we're going on a hike.

Love,
Cindy

"She sure is having fun," said Chuck.

Then Barry asked, "What did you get in the mail today, Chuck?"

"I got a letter from Mom and Dad telling me not to catch a cold. They're also sending something to keep the bugs away from me."

Just then, Mr. Stanley came over to the boys.

"Here's another letter for you, Barry."

Barry read his letter. The words were printed in green and were large. It said: "The Green Ghost will visit you tonight."

Barry was very surprised. But he was very happy about meeting a ghost. He kept on reading the letter over and over. Then he jumped up and down in front of the flagpole.

All day, Barry kept thinking only of the visit from the Green Ghost. Chuck was glad to see that his friend was so happy.

That night, Barry could not begin to fall asleep. He wanted to be awake when the Green Ghost came. But after a long time, Barry closed his eyes and fell asleep.

After a while, Barry felt something near him. He opened his eyes. It was a ghost! A real ghost! A *green* ghost!

He thought it would be best to be friends with ghosts, so he gave the Green Ghost a big cookie. Then, Barry and the ghost took a walk together. They walked and talked for a long time and they became good friends. Then the Green Ghost said that he wanted to go to sleep in Barry's tent. Both Barry and the Green Ghost fell asleep right away.

The next morning, when Barry opened his eyes, he saw that his friend the Green Ghost was gone. Barry ran out of his tent and looked all over. Then he walked to the flagpole.

There, he found Chuck sitting under the flag. Chuck was smiling and he was also eating a big cookie. The cookie was just like the one that Barry had given to the Green Ghost. Barry smiled at his friend.

"Did you see the Green Ghost?" Chuck asked Barry.

"Yes," said Barry with a big smile on his face. Chuck smiled, too, and gave his friend half of the big cookie.

Barry and Chuck at Camp

Preview Answer:

c. Barry got a postcard.

COMPREHENSION CHECK

Choose the best answer.

1. Barry and Chuck were
____a. at home in a tent.
____b. away at summer camp.
____c. at school.
____d. over at a friend's house playing a game.

2. The name of the place where Barry and Chuck were,was
____a. Two Trees.
____b. Bug City.
____c. Camp Tummy Too.
____d. Mr. Stanley's.

3. Barry got a letter from
____a. his mother and father.
____b. Mr. Stanley.
____c. his brother.
____d. the Green Ghost.

4. When Barry saw the big, green letters he was
____a. sad.
____b. happy.
____c. angry.
____d. scared.

5. The Green Ghost was
____a. friendly.
____b. mean.
____c. frightening.
____d. strong.

6. The Green Ghost came to the tent
____a. while Barry was awake.
____b. after Chuck went to sleep.
____c. before Mr. Stanley gave out the mail.
____d. after Barry fell asleep.

7. Chuck and the Green Ghost
____a. never met each other.
____b. did not like each other.
____c. were the same person.
____d. had met at another time.

8. Barry
____a. was sure that he saw a real ghost.
____b. knew that Chuck was the ghost.
____c. thought his sister had tricked him.
____d. wanted to go home right away.

9. Another name for this story could be
____a. "The Green Ghost."
____b. "Bug Spray."
____c. "Getting Letters."
____d. "Camp Life."

10. This story is mainly about
____a. going away to camp.
____b. seeing green ghosts.
____c. making a friend happy.
____d. eating big cookies.

Check your answers with the key on page 53.

Idea Starter: Tell about your first experiences away from home. Would you like to do it again? Why?

Barry and Chuck at Camp

VOCABULARY CHECK

asleep	begin	camp	flag	kept	mail

I. **Fill in the blank in each sentence with the right word from the box above.**

1. I will_____my piano lessons after school today.

2. I_____trying to get the ball in the basket.

3. Our_____is red, white and blue.

4. I sent my sister a letter in the_____.

5. We learn to swim and fish at_____.

6. The cat was_____on the chair.

II. **Fill in the blanks in the paragraph below with the right key words from the box above.**

Barry and Chuck slept in the same tent at_____. In the morning, Mr. Stanley called

them to the_____pole to get their_____. Barry got a letter from the Green

Ghost. That night,he could not_____to go to sleep because he_____thinking

about the ghost. When he finally fell_____, the Green Ghost came to his tent.

Check your answers with the key on page 56.

This page may be reproduced for classroom use.

Home Run

Learn the Key Words

print   (print)   a way of writing letters and words
Please print your name in the book.

radio   (rā ′ dē ō)   something that plays songs or brings news over the air
I like to listen to the radio before I go to sleep.

Saturday   (sat ′ ər dā)   a day of the week
There is no school on Saturday.

straight   (strāt)   not crooked; going one way
Sometimes I go straight home, but sometimes I stop at my friend's house.

use   (yüz)   do something with
Tom hoped it would snow so he could use his new sled.

you'll   (yül)   you will
I hope you'll have a very happy birthday.

Preview:
1. Read the title.
2. Look at the picture.
3. Read the first four paragraphs of the story.
4. Then answer the following question.

You learned from your preview that
_____a. it was raining very hard on Saturday morning.
_____b. Dan played ball with his friends only on Saturdays.
_____c. Dan liked to play ball, but he was not very good at it.
_____d. Dan told his mother that he would come home if it started to rain.

Turn to the Comprehension Check on page 24 for the right answer.

Now read the story.
Read to find out about a very exciting baseball game.

Home Run

Dan's team is on a winning streak and almost nothing will stop them.

Home Run

Playing ball was the one thing Dan loved best in all the world. He was good at it, too. He could run fast and catch a fly ball. He could hit the ball straight and far.

Each day after school, he would run outside to play ball. On Saturday, he played ball with his friends from morning to night. When he rode in the car, he listened to ball games on the radio.

One morning, as he got ready to go out, his mother said,"It looks like rain, Dan. The radio says it will rain, too. I hope you'll come straight home if it starts raining."

"Yes, I will come straight home," Dan said. "But I hope it does not rain. I wish it never rained on Saturdays because I like to play ball all day long."

His friend Jimmy came to the door. "Can we use your new ball, Dan?" he asked.

"Just as soon as I print my name on it," Dan said. He was happy to use his new ball in the game. But he did not want to lose it like his other ball.

"I hope I hit a home run," Jimmy said as they ran to the park together.

"I hope I do too," Dan shouted. He hoped to hit his new ball high and far. He wanted to run fast and reach home plate before the ball got there.

Many boys and girls came to the park that day. They ran and shouted. Dan made a great catch and got Amy out. That was good because Amy was one of the best players on the other team. Dan made many runs and had a wonderful time. But he hadn't hit the home run he wanted. And now it was his turn at bat, again.

"Maybe you'll get a home run this time," Jimmy called to him.

Dan felt a drop of rain on his nose and missed the ball that time. Just as the ball came by again, he felt another drop and missed. Now, he had just one more try.

"It's raining!" someone shouted as Dan got ready for his last try. In came the ball! and away it went! Dan ran as quickly as he could, all the way around to home plate.

"You did it!" shouted Jimmy. "You hit a home run, Dan!"

The rain was coming down harder and Dan's new ball was all wet. He would have to print his name on it again before the next game.

"How was the game?" his mother asked when he got home.

"Good," said Dan, "We all got home runs."

"All of you?" his mother asked, surprised.

"Yes," Dan laughed. "First, I hit a home run and then we all ran home!"

Home Run

COMPREHENSION CHECK

Choose the best answer.

1. The thing that Dan loved best in all the world was
____a. reading books.
____b. playing games.
____c. playing baseball.
____d. running on the track.

2. Dan printed his name on the ball so
____a. he could lend it to Jimmy.
____b. it wouldn't get mixed up.
____c. he could remember the game.
____d. it wouldn't get lost.

3. A home run in baseball is when a player
____a. runs home before the rain starts.
____b. runs around all the bases before the ball gets home.
____c. hits the ball and runs to one base.
____d. misses the ball three times in a row and has to leave.

4. Dan was glad that Amy got out because
____a. she was the first player up.
____b. he wanted to go home.
____c. he saw it was raining.
____d. she was a good player.

5. Dan missed the ball twice because
____a. drops of rain fell on his nose.
____b. he didn't see the ball.
____c. the sun was in his eyes.
____d. he didn't want to play.

6. Dan
____a. missed the ball three times.
____b. got a home run on his last try.
____c. went home early.
____d. gave his glove to Amy.

7. At the game on Saturday,
____a. Dan did not play ball well.
____b. the team did not play together.
____c. Dan played well.
____d. it was a bright sunny day.

8. Dan said all the children got home runs because they
____a. all had to run home when the rain started.
____b. all ran around the bases before the ball got home.
____c. all played very well.
____d. told him they did.

9. Another name for this story could be
____a. "A Rainy Day."
____b. "The Saturday Game."
____c. "Mother's Worries."
____d. "Jim's Friend."

10. This story is mainly about
____a. winning a baseball game.
____b. going to school on Saturdays.
____c. loving and playing baseball.
____d. living in the country.

Check your answers with the key on page 53.

Idea Starter: What do you think it would be like to be a famous ball player?

Home Run

VOCABULARY CHECK

print	radio	Saturday	straight	use	you'll

I. *Fill in the blank in each sentence with the right key word from the box above.*

1. The teacher will_____the spelling words on the board.

2. We do not go to school on_____.

3. If_____come to my house, we'll play a game.

4. My father always takes a_____on the boat.

5. We_____chalk and crayons to draw pictures.

6. My mother drove us_____to school.

II. *Fill in the blanks in the paragraph below with the right key words from the box above.*

Dan loved baseball. He listened to it on the_____and played in a game every_____.

He had to_____his name on his new ball before he could_____it in the game.

Dan wanted to hit the ball_____and make a home run. On Dan's last try, Jim shouted,

"Maybe_____hit one this time!" And Dan got his home run.

Check your answers with the key on page 57.

APRIL FOOL!

Learn the Key Words

beginning	(bi gin´ ng)	the start of something; the first part *Mary is <u>beginning</u> to like her new school now that she has made some friends there.*
butter	(but´ ər)	a thick, yellowish food made from milk; you spread it on bread *My mother went to the store to buy some <u>butter</u>.*
dad	(dad)	father *Fred's <u>dad</u> showed him how to catch fish.*
lucky	(luk´ ē)	bringing or having good luck *You were <u>lucky</u> to find the money that you lost.*
puddle	(pud´ l)	small pool of water *If you walk in a <u>puddle</u>, your feet will get wet.*
slowly	(slō´ lē)	taking one's time; the opposite of quickly *I like to eat ice cream <u>slowly</u>, so it lasts a long time.*

Preview:

1. Read the title.
2. Look at the picture.
3. Read the first ten paragraphs of the story.
4. Then answer the following question.

You learned from your preview that

_____a. Helen's mother played a trick on Mr. Turtle.
_____b. everyone plays tricks in April.
_____c. only children play tricks.
_____d. Robert put a frog on the butter.

Turn to the Comprehension Check on page 29 for the right answer.

Now read the story.

Read to find out about a fun day.

APRIL FOOL!

April Fool's Day is a time for fun and pranks all over the world.

Places You Will Read About:
France (fräns) a country in Europe
Scotland (skot′ lənd) a country of Great Britain, north of England

APRIL FOOL!

"Hello, Daddy," said Robert. "You look funny—you have something on your head."

"What is on my head?" asked his Dad.

"Your hair," said Robert. "April Fool!"

Robert's dad wanted to eat some bread and butter with his dinner, but there was a frog on the butter.

"April Fool!" said Robert again.

It was the first day of April, and children in many places were playing tricks.

Helen told her mother Mr. Turtle had called.

"I don't know a Mr. Turtle," said her mother, but she tried to call him.

"There is no Mr. Turtle here," a man told her, "This is the city zoo."

Then Helen's mother saw it was a trick—she was an April Fool.

On April 1st, Henry Smith was at work when a man told him, "Mrs. Smith called. She said you must hurry home at once."

Henry ran very fast to his house. But it was an April Fool's Day trick. Mrs. Smith had not called. But Henry was very lucky that he was an April Fool. When he got home, his house was on fire! He put out the fire very fast. He was just in time.

In France, an April Fool is called an April Fish. At the store, people buy cookies that look like fish. Children make funny pictures of fish and put these on their friends' clothes when the friends are not looking.

In Scotland, an April Fool is called an April Gowk. (A gowk is a funny-looking bird.) Bill and Tom live in Scotland. Bill asked his friend Tom to take a letter to Mr. Jones.

"You are lucky," said Bill, "Mr. Jones will give you some money."

So Tom took the letter, but Mr. Jones looked at it and said, "This letter is not for me. It is for Mrs. Wood. You are very lucky. She will give you some money."

Then Tom went to her.

Mrs. Wood looked at the letter and told him, "This letter is for Mr. Green. He will give you the money."

Many children play this trick in Scotland, and sometimes the boy takes all day looking for people to give the letter to. Then he slowly sees that it is a trick. He is an April Gowk.

Why do we play tricks on April 1st? Winter goes by slowly, but in April, the spring is beginning at last. The snow and ice are gone. People are beginning to go out more. They are happy, so they think of funny things to do.

April is a time for surprises. First, the sun comes out, and we take off our coats. Then it rains, and we put on our coats and step into a puddle. Then the sun is out again, and the puddles are gone; and then it rains again. The sun is playing tricks on us, and so is the rain. April is a time for tricks and games. April is a time to laugh.

APRIL FOOL!

COMPREHENSION CHECK

Choose the best answer.

1. Robert played a joke on his father because
____a. it was April Fool's Day.
____b. he was a funny boy.
____c. his father loved jokes.
____d. someone told him to.

2. Henry Smith was lucky he was an April Fool because he
____a. found the money he had lost.
____b. got to call Mrs. Smith on time.
____c. saved his house from burning down.
____d. learned how to play tricks on others.

3. In France, an April Fool is called an April
____a. Fly.
____b. Fish.
____c. Love.
____d. Joker.

4. In Scotland, an April Fool is named after a funny
____a. fish.
____b. man.
____c. cat.
____d. bird.

5. April Fool's Day
____a. does not mean anything.
____b. is only an American holiday.
____c. does not make people laugh.
____d. is a day of jokes and surprises.

6. People play tricks in April because
____a. they are sorry to see that winter is gone.
____b. it is the beginning of spring and they are happy.
____c. they want to make new friends.
____d. they want to forget their troubles.

7. The weather in April is always
____a. sunny.
____b. raining.
____c. changing.
____d. the same.

8. In many countries, April Fool's Day is a
____a. mean time.
____b. angry time.
____c. sad time.
____d. funny time.

9. Another name for this story could be
____a. "Spring is Coming."
____b. "The First Day of April."
____c. "Coats and Clothes."
____d. "Puddle Hopping."

10. This story is mainly about
____a. the children in France and Scotland.
____b. a man who saves his burning house.
____c. the jokes people play on April Fool's Day.
____d. a turtle with a name at the city zoo.

Check your answers with the key on page 53.

Idea Starter: What is your favorite April Fool's trick?

APRIL FOOL!

VOCABULARY CHECK

beginning	butter	dad	lucky	puddle	slowly

I. Fill in the blank in each sentence with the right key word from the box above.

1. I was_____to be the first in line at the movie.

2. After it rains,there is always a big_____in front of our house.

3. The_____of the book had many pictures.

4. My_____and I go to the park together.

5. I love lots of_____on my roll.

6. The turtle moved_____through the garden.

II. Match the key words in Column A with the right meaning in Column B. Write the letter on the line next to the key word.

A	**B**
_____ 1. lucky	a. the start of something
_____ 2. slowly	b. father
_____ 3. beginning	c. a small pool of water
_____ 4. dad	d. having good luck
_____ 5. butter	e. taking one's time
_____ 6. puddle	f. food you spread on bread

Check your answers with the key on page 57.

STANDING UP FOR ME

Learn the Key Words

basketball   (bas ′ kit bôl)   1.   a game played with a large ball and high net baskets
2.   the name of the ball used in the game
My father was a basketball player in high school.

build   (bild)   make something; put together
I will build a bird house for the robins.

ladder   (lad ′ ər)   two, big, wooden or metal poles with steps between them used for climbing
He climbed the ladder to reach the light bulb.

library   (lī ′ brer ē)   a building where books and papers are kept for people to read and borrow
You can read books at the library.

pay   (pā)   1.   give something in return for a job
I will pay you to cut my grass.
2.   worth the trouble
It does not pay to take the easy way.

soft   (sôft)   1.   easy to shape; not hard; smooth
The cat's fur was very soft.
2.   gentle and nice to hear, feel or taste
She sang in a soft voice.

Preview:

1.   Read the title.
2.   Look at the picture.
3.   Read the first six paragraphs of the story.
4.   Then answer the following question.

You learned from your preview that
____a. Matt was planning to leave home.
____b. Matt walked out in the middle of the basketball game.
____c. Matt's father was mad at him.
____d. Matt's father was hurt in an accident.

Turn to the Comprehension Check on page 34 for the right answer.

Now read the story.
Read to find out about a boy who discovers himself.

STANDING UP FOR ME

Matt learns that he is a very important person, and a very special one.

Some Things You Will Read About:
temper (tem′ pər) the way a person feels or behaves; one's mood
forever (fər ev′ ər) always; without ever coming to an end

STANDING UP FOR ME

"Are you going to sit on that ladder forever?"

"No," was all I said.

My temper had done it again. In the middle of a basketball game, I had gotten mad. I walked out on my team, on the coach, and my Dad.

Right now, I was sitting on the fire ladder outside of our apartment. It was my "thinking" spot. Today I had a lot to think about. Why did I always lose my temper? All it did was get me in trouble.

"Matt, I know Peter hurt your feelings today. But it doesn't pay to get so mad."

Dad was inside our apartment, a basketball in his hands. I knew he was hurt. His voice was soft.

As I started to answer, my hurt rushed back.

"He had no right to say 'Who *doesn't* like basketball?' Can he grow plants like I do? Does he build things for his mother like I do? Who wants to chase a dumb ball anyway?"

I stopped. I had lost my temper again. For a few seconds, my words hung in the air. Dad loved basketball and I didn't. It seemed that all of my troubles centered on that game.

I looked over at my plants. The window was filled with them. No one was better with plants, I thought proudly.

Dad's words floated out to me.

"No, Peter can't do the things you do, but he doesn't get mad either. What you did today was foolish, Matt. When will you learn to watch yourself?"

Dad was right about my temper, but wrong about me and basketball. I would never be the star he wanted me to be. That was *his* dream. But I had my own dreams. I reached over and ran a finger across a big, green leaf. It felt silky soft.

It was time I told Dad how I felt. I hoped he would understand.

"I'm sorry I made the team lose. I was wrong to leave. I know my playing means a lot to you. But it doesn't make *me* happy. I want to do something else."

I waited for a few seconds.

"I have a chance for a job over at the new library. The man who takes care of the trees and plants is looking for help. The job won't pay much, but I like the work. We may even build some benches."

"You really like working with plants, don't you?" Dad had stopped twisting the ball and stood listening to me.

I answered him quickly. "It's a chance for me to find out what I really can do. The garden man knows a lot. He teaches me things I could never learn from books."

"Do you ever go *into* the library or just work around it?"

I laughed. "Don't worry, I plan to go inside. There must be a book or two in there on basketball."

"Or plants," Dad said.

We laughed together. It was good to know he understood I had to be me.

STANDING UP FOR ME

COMPREHENSION CHECK

Choose the best answer.

Preview Answer:

b.   Matt walked out in the middle of a basketball game.

1. Matt was upset because
____a. his father had not come home yet.
____b. his father wanted him to go to the library.
____c. he lost his temper again.
____d. he had not gone to school.

2. Matt was feeling hurt because
____a. his father was angry at him.
____b. Peter did not understand his feelings.
____c. his mother did not like plants.
____d. he wasn't the captain of the team.

3. Dad's dream was for Matt to
____a. play basketball.
____b. study.
____c. grow plants.
____d. be a fireman.

4. What Matt did best was
____a. play basketball.
____b. make friends.
____c. stay quiet.
____d. grow plants.

5. Matt did the right thing when he
____a. became a basketball star.
____b. told his father how he felt.
____c. left the game angry.
____d. went up on the ladder.

6. Matt's Dad
____a. only wanted his son to play ball.
____b. did not care about what his son said.
____c. listened carefully to his son.
____d. asked his son to stay on the team.

7. Matt would learn about plants
____a. only from the garden man.
____b. from his father and his friends.
____c. only from books he read.
____d. from the garden man and books.

8. Matt
____a. knew a lot about himself.
____b. did not care about his father's feelings.
____c. did not know how he really felt about things.
____d. only wanted to have a lot of money.

9. Another name for this story could be
____a. "Different Dreams."
____b. "No Place For Matt."
____c. "Playing Ball."
____d. "Hiding Away."

10. This story is mainly about
____a. learning new things.
____b. talking about feelings and needs.
____c. having lots of friends.
____d. being liked by everyone.

Check your answers with the key on page 53.

Idea Starter: Have you ever had a problem that you wanted to talk over with your mother or father?
What was it?

STANDING UP FOR ME

VOCABULARY CHECK

basketball	build	ladder	library	pay	soft

I. *Fill in the blank in each sentence with the right key word from the box above.*

1. My neighbor said he would_____me for raking his leaves.

2. I held the_____while dad climbed to the top.

3. We play_____on the weekends.

4. My mother touched me with a_____hand.

5. I like to_____small tables and chairs.

6. The school_____has many kinds of books.

II. *Are the underlined words used the right way? Check yes or no.*

1. You don't have to pay for anything you buy. _____Yes _____No

2. When you build a doll house, people can live in it. _____Yes _____No

3. A ladder will help you get up to the roof. _____Yes _____No

4. Basketball is a game. _____Yes _____No

5. There are no books in the library. _____Yes _____No

6. A pillow feels soft. _____Yes _____No

Check your answers with the key on page 58.

Sara Sees the Town

Learn the Key Words

afraid   (ə frād′)   to be frightened
She is afraid of the dark.

anyone   (en′ ē wun)   any man, woman, or child
Does anyone know what time the movie starts?

chase   (chās)   to run after
When they play tag, the children chase after each other.

dollar   (dol′ ər)   a form of money in the United States
This toy costs one dollar.

held   (held)   had in your hands or arms; past tense of hold
Sue held the door open for the old woman.

line   (līn)   1.   a group of people or things
There was a line of people waiting to see the movie.
2.   a thin mark
A black line was drawn down the middle of the paper.

Preview:
1.   Read the title.
2.   Look at the picture.
3.   Read the first seven paragraphs of the story.
4.   Then answer the following question.

You learned from your preview that
_____a.   Sara's lunch was six cookies and an apple.
_____b.   Sara planned to take her dog with her.
_____c.   Jeff wasn't too happy about going to town.
_____d.   Jeff was the boy who lived next door.

Turn to the Comprehension Check on page 39 for the right answer.

Now read the story.
Read to find out what happens when Sara goes exploring.

Sara Sees the Town

Sara and Jeff have lots of fun when they take the day to see the town.

Sara Sees the Town

Sara put a lunch of five cookies and an apple in one bag. In another, she put a cookie and a bone. That would be her friend's lunch. Then, Sara went out to find her friend. She found him sleeping in the garden.

"Stop sleeping, Jeff!" she said.

Jeff sat up to look at Sara and his tail began to wag.

"Come on, you good old dog," said Sara, "let's go look around the town."

Jeff was happy to go along.

Sara held on to the lunches and a bottle of water. She had put a dollar in her pocket, too. A dollar could buy a lot.

She told Jeff, "If I forgot to bring something, we can buy it. We will have lots of fun today."

Sara didn't tell anyone she was going. She did not think anyone would mind.

Sara and Jeff walked for a long time. Soon, they found a park where they stopped to have lunch. Jeff had his bone and Sara had her apple. Each had water from the bottle. Then, Jeff found a ball and they played for a while.

When she went to eat the cookies, something was wrong. Sara lined them up but the number of cookies was not right. One of Sara's was gone. As she and Jeff ate their cookies, Sara saw a squirrel in a tree. He looked happy and he held the missing cookie!

Sara guessed it was time to go home, but something was wrong.

"Jeff, we are in trouble. I don't know where we are or how to get home," she said, "but don't be afraid, Jeff."

Jeff was no help. He just wanted to chase a frog who did not want to be chased.

Sara was not afraid of being lost. "I will just have to think of something to do," she said.

"I will call home! I know the number and I have money for the call."

She and Jeff walked to a store. Jeff sat by the door while she went in to make the call. There were some people there, so she stood on line. When she did get to the phone, she could not reach it. She looked around and found a box.

"I will step on this so I can reach it," she said. It worked just fine.

Soon, Sara was telling her mother and father the name of the store that she and Jeff were at. They would come for her and the dog in a little while. Then, Sara went out to Jeff.

She said, "They were happy that we are all right. But they were not happy that we went off without telling anyone. Something could have gone wrong for us, and no one would know. We could have been in big trouble!"

Then she laughed at Jeff. He was trying to make friends with another frog.

"It's a good thing you have me with you, Jeff. You don't know you are lost and you don't know how to call home!"

Sara Sees the Town

<table>
<tr><td>

Preview Answer:

b.   Sara planned to take her dog with her.
</td></tr>
</table>

COMPREHENSION CHECK

Choose the best answer.

1. Sara
____a. stayed at home and had a picnic.
____b. wanted to go on a short trip.
____ c. went to the park with her mother.
____d. shopped in a nearby store.

2. Jeff was Sara's
____a. dog.
____b. brother.
____ c. friend.
____d. cat.

3. Sara
____a. did not have to tell anyone about her trip.
____b. should have told someone where she was going.
____ c. knew her way around town.
____d. left Jeff at home fast asleep.

4. One of Sara's cookies was eaten by
____a. another little girl.
____b. Jeff.
____ c. a squirrel.
____d. a rabbit.

5. Sara and Jeff
____a. got home in time for dinner.
____b. did not like the park.
____ c. were chased by frogs.
____d. got lost on their trip.

6. When Sara knew she could not find her way, she
____a. got very worried.
____b. could not think of what to do.
____ c. kept her thoughts together.
____d. looked to Jeff for help.

7. Sara got help by
____a. calling out to a policeman.
____b. going to a store and phoning her parents.
____ c. following the same path home.
____d. asking another child to show them the way.

8. Jeff only cared about
____a. chasing frogs.
____b. getting home.
____ c. running away.
____d. eating cookies.

9. Another name for this story could be
____a. "Running Away."
____b. "Good Thinking."
____ c. "A Lovely Lunch."
____d. "Fun With Squirrels."

10. This story is mainly about
____a. going on a trip to the city.
____b. playing with a dog.
____ c. asking someone for help.
____d. what to do if one gets lost.

Check your answers with the key on page 53.

Idea Starter: If you were Sara's mother or father, what would you do when she returned home?

This page may be reproduced for classroom use.

Sara Sees the Town

VOCABULARY CHECK

afraid	anyone	chase	dollar	held	line

I. **Fill in the blank in each sentence with the right key word from the box above.**

1. Didn't _____ want to go to the game?

2. I drew a _____ on the ground so we could play hop scotch.

3. I was _____ to go outside by myself.

4. Karen _____ my books on the way home from school.

5. My brother had to _____ our dog until he caught him.

6. One _____ will buy us lunch.

II. **Fill in the puzzle using the key words from the box above.**

Across

1. any man, woman or child

3. to run after

5. money in the United States

Down

1. to be frightened

2. to have had in your hands

4. a thin mark

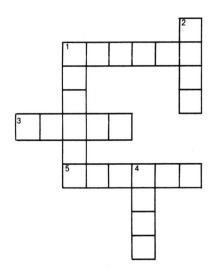

Check your answers with the key on page 58.

ONE NIGHT...

Learn the Key Words

flashlight   (flash ′ līt)   a light made to carry about
> *Ray takes a flashlight when he goes for a walk at night.*

hunter   (hun ′ tər)   someone who goes after animals
> *The hunter did not find any rabbits, so he had nothing to eat that night.*

number   (num ′ bər)   word which tells how many
> *The number of girls in the room was six.*

safe   (sāf)   not having to be afraid
> *Jenny felt safe playing in her own backyard.*

set   (set)   put; place
> *You can set the box down here.*

twelve   (twelv)   the number that is one more than eleven
> *Six dogs and six cats make twelve pets in all.*

Preview:
1. Read the title.
2. Look at the picture.
3. Read the first three paragraphs of the story.
4. Then answer the following question.

You learned from your preview that
____a. the hunter is a very brave man.
____b. the hunter does not like the quiet.
____c. the hunter is afraid of the dark.
____d. the hunter wants the wolf as a pet.

Turn to the Comprehension Check on page 44 for the right answer.

Now read the story.

Read to find out about a hunter who cares about life in the forest.

ONE NIGHT...

What is really the difference between man and animals? Could it be freedom?

ONE NIGHT...

The hunter stops to listen. All is quiet, but he knows it is out there. He has heard the sound and knows it cannot be far away.

The night is very dark. Nothing looks like it does in the day. He is glad he has his flashlight. He has never been afraid of an animal and he is not afraid now. But he needs the light to help him find his way.

For a long time, he walks through the tall trees. He is almost ready to give up, when he hears the sound again. It's the cry of a wolf. It is so near that he stops right where he is. Careful to make no noise, he takes time to set down his things. He puts down the flashlight, too, because a light will make the wolf run away. He wants to see this wolf. He wants to take this wolf home with him. That will show what a great hunter he is.

Slowly now, he walks on a little way. When he comes near the lake, he stops. From a safe place in the trees, he can just see what is going on. And what he sees is so wonderful, he almost lets out a shout.

There is not just one wolf, but a large number of them. First, he sees the eight big ones, and then, four little ones. There are twelve in all.

He knows he will have just one try to get a wolf, for the noise will start the others running. But he is in no hurry. He will wait for everything to be just right.

The animals are hard to see in the dark, but he can just make them out. One big wolf, its head held high, looks like a king. Maybe it is the king of the pack. When it walks by, the others move out of its way. That is the one the hunter wants.

He is not afraid there in the dark. He feels safe, because most animals will run away from people. A wolf, too, will run if it can. Twelve of them together will run from one man.

Another wolf comes up to the leader. The hunter can tell she is a mother wolf, for her little ones come, too. The two big ones make no noise at all. But it looks like they are talking, talking without words in some strange way that people could never understand.

Now is the time. But the hunter does nothing. For a long time, he just sits there. Then, he returns quietly to where he set down his things.

Twelve was the number that came to the lake. And twelve will go away. The hunter will go to his tent and sleep. Many times after this, he will think of the wolf king. How glad he is that he is living in this wonderful world of animals.

ONE NIGHT...

COMPREHENSION CHECK

Choose the best answer.

1. This story takes place
____a.   in a park.
____b.   in the dark woods.
____ c.   at a picnic.
____d.   in the rain.

2. The hunter is helped to find his way by
____a.   looking carefully.
____b.   feeling the trees.
____ c.   using a flashlight.
____d.   listening to noises.

3. In order to show what a good hunter he is, the man wants to
____a.   take a wolf home with him.
____b.   track and kill a deer.
____ c.   make a path through the woods.
____d.   capture a grizzly bear.

4. By the lake, the hunter finds
____a.   a wolf family.
____b.   one big wolf.
____ c.   many other hunters.
____d.   a dead wolf.

5. The wolf that held its head high was
____a.   the mother of the wolf family.
____b.   killed by the hunter.
____ c.   the head of the wolf family.
____d.   a member of another family.

6. The mother wolf and the king wolf
____a.   did not like each other.
____b.   went two different ways.
____ c.   watched the young ones run away.
____d.   talked to each other without using words.

7. The hunter
____a.   could have killed the king wolf.
____b.   never would have reached the king wolf.
____ c.   never thought of killing the king wolf.
____d.   was sorry he had not killed the king wolf.

8. The hunter changed his mind because
____a.   he was tired and wanted to go to sleep.
____b.   he saw how beautiful and important the wolf family was.
____ c.   the king wolf ran to get help.
____d.   the mother wolf ran away with her children.

9. Another name for this story could be
____a.   "Waiting to Kill at Midnight."
____b.   "The Hunter Makes Up His Mind."
____ c.   "The Woods at Night."
____d.   "A Trip to the Lake."

10. This story is mainly about
____a.   a trip through the woods.
____b.   hunting at night.
____ c.   seeing the beauty in an animal.
____d.   sleeping in a tent.

Check your answers with the key on page 53.

Idea Starter: Would you have acted the same way as the hunter? Explain.

ONE NIGHT...

VOCABULARY CHECK

flashlight	hunter	number	safe	set	twelve

I. Fill in the blank in each sentence with the right key word from the box above.

1. I feel_____in my room.

2. The_____of animals in the zoo is ten.

3. _____is two more than ten.

4. I turned on my_____so I could find my way to the kitchen.

5. The_____could not kill the wolf.

6. John_____his books on the table.

II. Match the key words in Column A with the right meaning in Column B. Write the letter on the line next to the key word.

	A		B
_____ 1.	flashlight	a.	one more than eleven
_____ 2.	number	b.	put
_____ 3.	hunter	c.	a light carried about
_____ 4.	set	d.	not having to be afraid
_____ 5.	twelve	e.	word which tells how many
_____ 6.	safe	f.	someone who goes after animals

Check your answers with the key on page 59.

Lost and Found

Learn the Key Words

elevator	(el′ə vā tər)	a large, box-like machine that carries people up and down so they don't have to use the stairs *John likes to visit the place where his father works so he can ride in the elevator.*
glove	(gluv)	a covering for the hand *Cathy kept one hand in her pocket because she had lost her glove.*
haven't	(hav′ ənt)	have not *We haven't gone to the zoo once this year.*
key	(kē)	something that fits into a door to let people in or out (cars have keys, too, to make them start) *Ann can't go in the house because she does not have her key.*
leave	(lēv)	go away from *Our train will leave the station very soon.*
tie	(tī)	make things stay together, as with strings *Andy wants a long string to tie his balloon to the wagon.*

Preview:
1. Read the title.
2. Look at the picture.
3. Read the first three paragraphs of the story.
4. Then answer the following question.

You learned from your preview that
____a. Mrs. O'Leary lived in Ireland until she died.
____b. Mrs. O'Leary had a coat to match her green gloves.
____c. Mrs. O'Leary's little green glove was said to be lucky.
____d. Ruby was really Mrs. O'Leary's daughter.

Turn to the Comprehension Check on page 49 for the right answer.

Now read the story.
Read to find out about a real lucky charm.

Lost and Found

Mrs. O'Leary made up the tale about the little people and the green glove. Didn't she?

A Place You Will Read About:
Ireland (īr ′ lənd)   one of the British Isles

Lost and Found

When Mrs. O'Leary was a little girl, she lived far away in a land called Ireland. Her name was not Mrs. O'Leary then. She was called Kitty.

When she had to leave Ireland to come to America, she could not bring much with her. But she did bring her little green glove. There was just one glove, too tiny to fit anyone. She had found it one day in the grass. Some people said it would make her lucky. They said one of the tiny, magic people who live in Ireland must have lost it.

Now, Mrs. Kitty O'Leary was a grown woman who lived in a big house with an elevator. One of the other people who lived there was a girl named Ruby. And another was a man named Mr. Brown.

One day, when Ruby stopped to tie her shoe, she heard Mr. Brown say, "Oh, no, I must have lost it. My key was in my pocket when I left my room," he said. "But now I haven't got it."

"Maybe we can find it, Mr. Brown," said Ruby.

They looked all around, but found nothing. At last, Mr. Brown had to leave to go to work. Ruby kept on looking, but she could not find that key.

From a window high up in the house, Ruby's mother called her to come and eat. Slowly, Ruby walked inside and into the elevator. She did not know what Mr. Brown was going to do without his key.

Then she saw that she had to tie her shoe.

"Not again!" she said. And then the elevator stopped so fast that it knocked her over. "That does it!" Ruby shouted. "Everything is going wrong!"

But then she saw something strange in the corner. It was a tiny, green glove; so tiny it would not fit anyone. And there, right under it, was a key. She knew right away it must be Mr. Brown's. But where did that little glove come from?

It did not take Ruby long to find Mrs. O'Leary. But Mrs. O'Leary was very surprised.

"I don't think I took the glove out of my room," she said.

She told Ruby how she had found the glove when she was a girl and about the little magic people of Ireland.

"Do you think there are little people here, too?" Ruby asked.

"If there are, I haven't heard about them," Mrs. O'Leary said. "I do not think there are any little people at all. Do you?"

"I guess not," Ruby said.

But she never did learn how that funny, little green glove had come to be right there on Mr. Brown's lost key.

Lost and Found

COMPREHENSION CHECK

Choose the best answer.

1. Mrs. O'Leary came from
____a. England.
____b. France.
____c. Ireland.
____d. Italy.

2. In the grass, Mrs. O'Leary found
____a. magic people.
____b. a little green glove.
____c. a small stone.
____d. a lost key.

3. People said that the glove
____a. would bring bad luck.
____b. would bring money.
____c. was left behind by a small child.
____d. was lost by a tiny, magic person.

4. Mr. Brown lost his
____a. key.
____b. way.
____c. glove.
____d. money.

5. In the elevator,
____a. Ruby found a little green glove and the key.
____b. Ruby saw some tiny, magic people.
____c. Mr. Brown found his lost key.
____d. Mrs. O'Leary lost her tiny, green glove and key.

6. If the elevator had not stopped suddenly, Ruby
____a. would have been badly hurt.
____b. would have found the money anyway.
____c. might not have discovered the glove.
____d. might not have tied her shoe.

7. The little green glove in the elevator
____a. belonged to Ruby's mother.
____b. belonged to Mrs. Brown.
____c. was the same one that Mrs. O'Leary found in Ireland.
____d. did not belong to anyone in the building.

8. Mrs. O'Leary and Ruby
____a. believed in the magic men.
____b. knew who had left the glove.
____c. were puzzled by what had happened.
____d. went back to Ireland to learn the truth.

9. Another name for this story could be
____a. "Mr. Brown's Key."
____b. "The Little People."
____c. "Ruby's Mother."
____d. "The Elevator."

10. This story is mainly about
____a. people who believe in magic.
____b. the elevator in a large building.
____c. some strange happenings.
____d. three strange people.

Check your answers with the key on page 53.

Idea Starter: What lucky charms do you have? Do you have any proof that they are lucky?

Lost and Found

VOCABULARY CHECK

elevator	glove	haven't	key	leave	tie

I. *Fill in the blank in each sentence with the right key word from the box above.*

1. Susan lost her_____on her way to school.

2. I got off the_____at the fourth floor.

3. My father turned the_____and started the car.

4. I always_____my books together so I won't lose them.

5. I _____ been to the playground today.

6. We had to_____the classroom during the fire drill.

II. *Fill in the blanks in the story with the key words from the box above. One of the key words is used twice.*

Mr. Brown had to_____for work so Ruby kept looking for his lost_____.
She got into the_____and bent down to_____her shoe. Suddenly, the elevator
stopped and Ruby fell over. In the corner, she saw a little green _____ and the missing
_____. "I _____ any idea how it got there!" exclaimed Mrs. O'Leary.

Check your answers with the key on page 59.

KEY WORDS
Lessons B-21 — B-30

B-21

quick
race
rode
sled
start
station

B-22

quiet
ring
sell
skate
suppose
teach

B-23

afternoon
between
careful
eight
kick
magic

B-24

asleep
begin
camp
flag
kept
mail

B-25

print
radio
Saturday
straight
use
you'll

B-26

beginning
butter
dad
lucky
puddle
slowly

KEY WORDS
Lessons B-21 — B-30

B-27

basketball
build
ladder
library
pay
soft

B-28

afraid
anyone
chase
dollar
held
line

B-29

flashlight
hunter
number
safe
set
twelve

B-30

elevator
glove
haven't
key
leave
tie

COMPREHENSION CHECK ANSWER KEY
Lessons B-21 — B-30

LESSON NUMBER	QUESTION NUMBER										PAGE NUMBER
	1	2	3	4	5	6	7	8	9	10	
B-21	b	(c)	d	a	a	c	b	a	△b	☐b	4
B-22	b	c	d	(a)	b	d	d	b	△a	☐a	9
B-23	b	c	(b)	d	a	c	d	(a)	△b	☐c	14
B-24	b	c	d	b	a	d	(c)	(b)	△a	☐c	19
B-25	c	d	b	d	a	b	(c)	a	△b	☐c	24
B-26	a	c	b	d	d	b	c	(d)	△b	☐c	29
B-27	c	b	a	d	(b)	c	d	(a)	△a	☐b	34
B-28	b	a	(b)	c	d	(c)	b	a	△b	☐d	39
B-29	b	c	a	a	c	d	(a)	(b)	△b	☐c	44
B-30	c	b	d	a	a	(c)	c	(c)	△b	☐c	49

Code: ◯ = Inference
       △ = Another Name for the Selection
       ☐ = Main Idea

NOTES

VOCABULARY CHECK ANSWER KEY
Lessons B-21 — B-30

I.
1. station
2. quick
3. sled
4. race
5. start
6. rode

II.
1. start
2. rode
3. station
4. sled
5. race
6. quick

I.
1. ring
2. quiet
3. suppose
4. sell
5. teach
6. skate

II.

VOCABULARY CHECK ANSWER KEY
Lessons B-21 — B-30

LESSON
NUMBER

PAGE
NUMBER

B-23 **THE SECRET OF THE MAGIC WATER**   15

I. 1. afternoon   *II.* 1. yes
    2. careful   2. no
    3. Eight   3. no
    4. kick   4. yes
    5. between   5. no
    6. magic   6. yes

B-24 **BARRY AND CHUCK AT CAMP**   20

I. 1. begin   *II.* 1. camp
    2. kept   2. flag
    3. flag   3. mail
    4. mail   4. begin
    5. camp   5. kept
    6. asleep   6. asleep

56

VOCABULARY CHECK ANSWER KEY
Lessons B-21 — B-30

B-25 HOME RUN   25

I. 1. print
2. Saturday
3. you'll
4. radio
5. use
6. straight

II. 1. radio
2. Saturday
3. print
4. use
5. straight
6. you'll

B-26 APRIL FOOL!   30

I. 1. lucky
2. puddle
3. beginning
4. dad
5. butter
6. slowly

II. 1. d
2. e
3. a
4. b
5. f
6. c

VOCABULARY CHECK ANSWER KEY
Lessons B-21 — B-30

LESSON NUMBER		PAGE NUMBER

B-27   STANDING UP FOR ME   35

I.   1.   pay
       2.   ladder
       3.   basketball
       4.   soft
       5.   build
       6.   library

II. 1.   no
       2.   no
       3.   yes
       4.   yes
       5.   no
       6.   yes

B-28   SARA SEES THE TOWN   40

I.   1.   anyone
       2.   line
       3.   afraid
       4.   held
       5.   chase
       6.   dollar

II.

58

VOCABULARY CHECK ANSWER KEY
Lessons B-21 — B-30

B-29 ONE NIGHT . . .

I.
1. safe
2. number
3. Twelve
4. flashlight
5. hunter
6. set

II.
1. c
2. e
3. f
4. b
5. a
6. d

B-30 LOST AND FOUND

I.
1. glove
2. elevator
3. key
4. tie
5. haven't
6. leave

II.
1. leave
2. key
3. elevator
4. tie
5. glove
6. key
7. haven't

NOTES